www.booksbyboxer.com

Bee Three Publishing is an imprint of Books By Boxer
Published by
Books By Boxer, Leeds, LS13 4BS UK
Books by Boxer (EU), Dublin D02 P593 IRELAND
© Books By Boxer 2023
All Rights Reserved
**MADE IN MALTA**
ISBN: 9781915410153

This book is produced from responsibly sourced paper to ensure forest management

# MAUD STEVENS WAGNER

FEBRUARY 12TH, 1877 – JANUARY 30TH, 1961

KANSAS, USA.

## The first female tattoo artist.

WHILST WORKING AS A CONTORTIONIST AND AERIALIST ACROSS TRAVELLING CIRCUSES, SHE MET HER LATE HUSBAND GUS WAGNER (SELF-PROCLAIMED "THE MOST ARTISTICALLY MARKED UP MAN IN AMERICA").

SHE EXCHANGED A ROMANTIC DATE WITH GUS FOR A LESSON IN TATTOOING, AND SOME YEARS LATER, BECAME THE UNITED STATES' FIRST KNOWN FEMALE TATTOO ARTIST, OPENING UP THE INDUSTRY FOR MORE WOMEN TO LEARN THE ART AND FOLLOW THEIR DREAMS AND DESIRES OF BECOMING A FEMALE TATTOO ARTIST.

MAUD ALSO HELPED MAKE IT MORE SOCIALLY ACCEPTABLE FOR WOMEN TO DON A TATTOO OF THEIR OWN - PAVING THE WAY FOR NEW STYLES!

DESPITE THE INVENTION OF THE TATTOO MACHINE IN 1891, MAUD AND HER HUSBAND WERE TWO OF THE LAST TATTOO ARTISTS TO WORK SOLELY BY HAND TO GIVE TRADITIONAL HAND POKED TATTOOS.

# ELIZABETH SEAMAN

MAY 5TH, 1864 – JANUARY 27TH, 1922

PENNSYLVANIA, USA.

## Investigative journalist who faked her way into an asylum.

DETERMINED TO EXPOSE THE DREADFUL TREATMENT OF PATIENTS, THIS FEARLESS HEROINE FAKED HER WAY INTO AN ASYLUM!

IN 1885, ELIZABETH LANDED A JOB AT THE PITTSBURGH DISPATCH UNDER THE PENNAME 'NELLIE BLY'. WRITING ABOUT WOMEN'S RIGHTS, AND THE LIVES AND CUSTOMS OF MEXICAN CIVILIANS, LED TO HER BEING HARASSED AND THREATENED WITH ARREST.

SHE WENT ON TO EXPOSE THE ABUSE WITHIN THE WOMEN'S LUNATIC ASYLUM BY GOING UNDERCOVER! SHE REFUSED TO SLEEP AND ACTED DERANGED TO FAKE HER WAY IN!

ELIZABETH FOUND HERSELF IN A LIVING HELL – EXPERIENCING CRUEL TORTURE AND ABUSE FIRST-HAND.

ELIZABETH WAS RELEASED 10 DAYS LATER WITH THE HELP OF LAWYERS, AND SHE GOT TO WORK, WRITING HER REPORT ON HER EXPERIENCES, AND THOSE OF THE WOMEN WHO SURROUNDED HER, WHICH IMPLEMENTED REFORMATION OF THE INSTITUTE.

# AMELIA EARHART

JULY 24TH, 1897 - JULY 2ND, 1937

KANSAS, USA.

## First woman to fly solo across the Atlantic.

A REBEL NOT ONLY IN THE SKIES, AMELIA EARHART IS POSSIBLY THE MOST WELL-KNOWN FEMALE PILOT, KNOWN FOR HER CARE-FREE, DARING ATTITUDE AND HER WILL-POWER TO OVERCOME EVERY OBSTACLE SHE FACED!

AMELIA HAD A SENSE OF DEFIANT ADVENTURE FROM THE VERY BEGINNING, AND AFTER MAKING A HOMEMADE ROLLERCOASTER, FELL IN LOVE WITH THE IDEA OF FLYING!

LEARNING HOW TO FLY IN HER TWENTIES, IT WAS ONLY IN HER EARLY THIRTIES WHEN SHE SET OFF TO FLY SOLO OVER THE ATLANTIC OCEAN, SETTING A NEW WORLD RECORD FOR WOMEN-KIND!

BEFORE HER MYSTERIOUS DISAPPEARANCE WHILE FLYING IN 1937, SHE WOULD SET MANY RECORDS FOR WOMEN, AND WOULD INSPIRE WOMEN TO BREAK THE MOLD AND DO SOMETHING REBELLIOUS IN THEIR LIVES!

"Women, like men, should try to do the impossible. And when they fail, their failure should be a challenge to others."

- Amelia Earhart

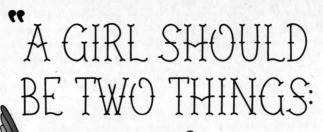

"A GIRL SHOULD
BE TWO THINGS:

*Who*

AND

*What*

SHE WANTS."

- COCO CHANEL

# Be intentional

**BE INTENTIONAL** WITH YOUR CAREER GROWTH! SOMETIMES IT'S ALL TOO EASY TO SAY WHERE YOU WANT TO BE IN 5 YEARS' TIME BUT NOT ACTUALLY TAKE THE STEPS TO ACT.

START BY **CREATING MANAGEABLE GOALS.** WHAT IS SOMETHING YOU CAN ACHIEVE THIS MONTH? CREATE A LIST OR VISUALIZE THEM BY PLOTTING INTO A CALENDAR.

**GIVE YOURSELF REALISTIC TIMELINES** – MOST OFTEN YOUR DREAM JOB WON'T BE OFFERED TO YOU OVERNIGHT. IT TAKES TIME TO BUILD SKILLS AND GROW YOUR CONFIDENCE, BUT WITH EACH DAY, MONTH, OR YEAR YOU'RE ONE STEP CLOSER.

BEING INTENTIONAL WITH YOUR CAREER GROWTH ALSO INCLUDES **CHECKING IN ON YOURSELF.** IDENTIFY WHAT IS WORKING AND WHAT'S NOT WORKING. BY KNOWING YOUR OWN HOLD BACKS IT ALLOWS YOU TO ADJUST YOUR PATH AROUND THOSE ROAD BLOCKS.

NO BADASS WOMEN ACHIEVED THEIR GREATNESS BY SITTING BACK AND WATCHING. EACH WOMEN HAD A CLEAR GOAL AND DIDN'T LET ANYTHING GET IN THEIR WAY OF ACHIEVING IT!

## DOROTHY LAWRENCE

OCTOBER 4TH, 1896 – OCTOBER 4TH, 1964
MIDDLESEX, ENGLAND.

# Posed as a male soldier to report from the WWI frontline.

DOROTHY LAWRENCE WAS AN ENGLISH JOURNALIST WHO REPORTED FROM THE FRONT LINE IN WORLD WAR I! THE ONLY ISSUE WAS THAT THEY DIDN'T ALLOW WOMEN ON THE FRONTLINE, BUT INSTEAD OF ACCEPTING DEFEAT, DOROTHY MADE HER WAY TO THE TRENCHES DISGUISED AS A MAN!

UNDER THE ALIAS 'PRIVATE DENIS SMITH', DOROTHY IS STILL THE ONLY REPORTED WOMAN TO HAVE BEEN ON THE FRONTLINE DURING WORLD WAR I!

ONCE HER IDENTITY WAS REVEALED, SHE WAS SWIFTLY ARRESTED, AND LATER RELEASED ONTO THE VERY SAME FERRY THAT EMMELINE PANKHURST WAS ON, AND ACTUALLY ASKED HER TO SPEAK ABOUT HER EXPERIENCES AT A SUFFRAGETTE MEETING!

DR. ELIZABETH BLACKWELL

FEBRUARY 3RD, 1821 – MAY 31ST, 1910

BRISTOL, ENGLAND.

# First woman registered in the General Medical Council.

NOT ONLY DID SHE BECOME THE FIRST WOMAN IN AMERICA TO BE QUALIFIED AS A DOCTOR, DR. ELIZABETH BLACKWELL FOUGHT BACK AGAINST HER MISOGYNISTIC MALE PEERS, PROVING THEM WRONG!

ONE OF THE MOST INFLUENTIAL WOMEN IN MEDICAL HISTORY, DR. ELIZABETH BLACKWELL WAS ALSO THE FIRST TO HAVE HER NAME ADDED INTO THE BRITISH GENERAL MEDICAL COUNCIL'S MEDICAL REGISTER.

AFTER MOVING TO AMERICA AT 17, A FAMILY FRIEND BECAME TERMINALLY ILL, AND SHE BECAME DETERMINED TO BECOME A PHYSICIAN, AND APPLYING TO MANY MEDICAL COLLEGES ACROSS AMERICA.

SHE FOUND HERSELF BRUTALLY REJECTED BY ALL BUT ONE COLLEGE BECAUSE OF HER GENDER, AND THE ONE WHO ALLOWED HER TO JOIN DID SO AS A CRUEL JOKE BETWEEN MALE STUDENTS. FACING PREJUDICE AND SEXISM TO NO END, SHE FOUGHT TIRELESSLY TO RECEIVE HER M.D. DEGREE, INFLUENCING HER SISTER AND MANY OTHER WOMEN TO DO THE SAME!

"IF THEY DON'T
GIVE YOU A
Seat
AT THE TABLE,
BRING A
Folding chair."

— SHIRLEY CHISHOLM

# Know your worth

IT MAY BE TRUE WHAT THEY SAY, THAT WOMEN SOMETIMES WORK TWICE AS HARD FOR HALF AS MUCH! BUT IT'S TIME THIS ENDS - **KNOW YOUR WORTH, AND DEMAND IT!**

IT'S TIME TO MAKE CHANGE AND CARVE OUT YOUR OWN SPACE, EVEN IF THAT SEEMS LIKE AN UPHILL STRUGGLE. IF YOU FEEL THAT YOU ARE BEING UNDERSOLD IN YOUR JOB, OR NOT RESPECTED ENOUGH, THEN IT'S TIME TO VOICE YOUR CONCERNS!

FOR CENTURIES, WOMEN HAVE BEEN FORCED TO SIT BACK AND WATCH OPPORTUNITIES BE HANDED TO MEN, EVEN THOUGH THEY ARE MORE QUALIFIED.

**DEMAND TO BE RESPECTED,** AND KNOW YOUR WORTH IN THE WORKPLACE! BEING A STRONG WOMAN IN THE WORKPLACE MAY SEEM INTIMIDATING, BUT IN ORDER TO SEE THE CHANGE YOU WANT TO SEE IN YOUR CAREER FIELD, ESPECIALLY FOR YOUR FEMALE PEERS, **SOMETIMES YOU NEED TO BE THE CHANGE!**

# PIA KLEMP

OCTOBER 10TH, 1983

BEUEL, GERMANY.

## Rescued migrants in the Mediterranean.

PIA KLEMP IS A BADASS GERMAN BIOLOGIST AND SEA CAPTAIN, WHO USED HER RESOURCES TO HELP RESCUE OVER 1000 MIGRANTS, WHO WERE AT RISK OF DROWNING IN THE TREACHEROUS MEDITERRANEAN SEA!

JOINING A MARINE CONSERVATION ORGANIZATION IN 2011, SHE WORKED HARD TO GAIN HER SEA CAPTAIN'S LICENSE. WHEN THE 2015 MIGRANT CRISIS BEGAN, PIA KNEW SHE HAD TO DO SOMETHING, AND WAS DETERMINED TO HELP A GERMAN ORGANIZATION 'SEA-WATCH', BY CAPTAINING A SHIP TO HELP RESCUE MIGRANTS.

WHILST THE ACTION IS PROTECTED BY THE 1982 UNITED NATIONS LAW OF THE SEA, SHE KNEW THERE WAS A DANGER OF CONVICTION. DUE TO A CRACKDOWN ON MIGRANTS TRAVELLING IN THE MEDITERRANEAN, THOSE FOUND HELPING THEM WERE CHARGED WITH "ASSISTING ILLEGAL IMMIGRATION".

DESPITE THESE RISKS, HER ACT OF REBELLION AGAINST THE LAW SAVED OVER 1000 AT-RISK MIGRANTS FROM DROWNING! SHE NOW FACES UP TO 20 YEARS IN PRISON, BUT STILL STANDS BY HER ACTIONS, AND WOULD DO IT ALL AGAIN.

# ANNETTE KELLERMAN

JULY 6TH, 1886 – NOVEMBER 6TH, 1975
MARRICKVILLE, AUSTRALIA.

## First woman to wear a one piece swimsuit.

THE AUSTRALIAN SWIMMER, FILM ACTRESS AND WRITER ALREADY HAS A PRETTY BADASS JOB HISTORY! WHAT SHE GOES DOWN IN HISTORY FOR, HOWEVER, IS BEING THE FIRST WOMAN TO WEAR A ONE-PIECE SWIMSUIT!

BEFORE KELLERMAN, WOMEN WERE ONLY ALLOWED TO WEAR PANTALOONS, IN ORDER TO PROTECT THEIR MODESTY. HOWEVER, KELLERMAN TOOK A STAND AND PROUDLY POSED IN HER ONE PIECE!

BELIEVE IT OR NOT, KELLERMAN WAS ACTUALLY ARRESTED FOR INDECENT EXPOSURE IN 1907 DUE TO COMPLAINTS FROM THE PUBLIC. HOWEVER, HER ACTION AND DETERMINATION TO WEAR A ONE PIECE HAD ALREADY TRIGGERED A TIDAL WAVE OF WOMEN WHO WERE BEGINNING TO TAKE CHARGE OF THEIR OWN BODY AND DO THE SAME!

"He asked me
'What's your favourite
POSITION?'
I said
'CEO.'"

- LAUREN CONRAD

# Surround yourself with love

**CUT OUT NEGATIVE ENERGY!** BY HAVING PEOPLE IN YOUR LIFE THAT BOOST YOU UP, AND RECOGNIZING THE PEOPLE THAT DRAG YOU DOWN, YOU'LL HAVE FAR MORE SELF-LOVE, PRIDE AND CONFIDENCE IN YOURSELF!

**GIVE OUT POSITIVITY** - LET YOUR FRIENDS AND FAMILY KNOW HOW MUCH YOU VALUE THEIR PRESENCE, AND ENCOURAGE THAT IN OTHER PEOPLE.

ON THE FLIP SIDE, RECOGNIZE THOSE INDIVIDUALS WHO DRAG YOU DOWN, AND DON'T PROVIDE A POSITIVE INFLUENCE IN YOUR LIFE. DON'T FEEL GUILTY ABOUT REMOVING SUCH PEOPLE FROM YOUR DAILY LIFE... **ENERGY FEEDS ENERGY, SO WHY NOT MAKE IT POSITIVE?!**

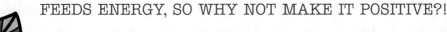

# ELIZABETH ECKFORD

OCTOBER 4TH, 1941

LITTLE ROCK, USA.

## Part of the Little Rock Nine.

FEARLESS AND DETERMINED TO STICK IT TO THE RACISTS IN HER TOWN, ELIZABETH ECKFORD IS ONE BADASS! A MEMBER OF THE LITTLE ROCK NINE, THE FIRST AFRICAN AMERICAN STUDENTS TO ATTEMPT TO DESEGREGATE LITTLE ROCK CENTRAL HIGH SCHOOL.

ON SEPTEMBER 3RD, 1957 AT THE AGE OF JUST 15, ELIZABETH ANN ECKFORD ARRIVED AT LITTLE ROCK CENTRAL HIGH SCHOOL, ALONE, AND WAS FACED WITH AN ANGRY MOB OF RACISTS WHO WERE PROTESTING OUTSIDE OF THE SCHOOL! INSTEAD OF TURNING BACK, ELIZABETH PUT ON HER SUNGLASSES AND WALKED TO THE SCHOOL WITH HER HEAD HELD HIGH!

ENDURING VERBAL AND PHYSICAL ABUSE THROUGHOUT HER TIME AT THE SCHOOL, FROM BOTH PARENTS AND TEACHERS, ELIZABETH ECKFORD COMPLETED HER STUDIES, AS A FINAL WAY TO TELL THE RACISTS WHO WERE AGAINST HER, WHERE TO SHOVE IT!

# ANNIE OAKLEY

AUGUST 13TH, 1860 – NOVEMBER 3RD, 1926

OHIO, USA.

## Legendary American markswoman and sharpshooter.

'AMERICA'S SWEETHEART'...IF SHE HAD A MASSIVE GUN AND SUPER SHARP AIM! ANNIE OAKLEY IS ONE OF THE MOST FAMOUS SHARPSHOOTERS IN THE HISTORY OF THE WILD WEST!

BEATING MEN AT THEIR OWN GAME, SHE QUICKLY ROSE TO FAME AS THE BEST MARKSWOMEN AND SHARPSHOOTER AROUND, AND ON THANKSGIVING IN 1875, ANNIE OAKLEY SHOWED THE WORLD WHO WAS BOSS BY BEATING THE MOST LEGENDARY MARKSMAN OF THE TIME, FRANK BUTLER.

TEACHING MEN NEVER TO JUDGE A BOOK BY ITS COVER, ANNIE OAKLEY PROVED THAT WHATEVER MEN CAN DO, WOMEN CAN DO BETTER! OAKLEY DOMINATED AN ALMOST ALL-MALE FIELD, SHOWING THAT YOU CAN DO WHATEVER YOU SET YOUR MIND TO WITH DETERMINATION, PASSION, AND A REALLY BIG GUN!

"I AM A WOMAN

*Phenomenally.*

PHENOMENAL
WOMAN, THATS
*Me.*"

- MAYA ANGELOU

# Support other women

WOMEN SHARE A COLLECTIVE STRUGGLE IN A MALE-DOMINATED WORLD, AND ARE USED TO TAKING ON MUCH MORE THAN THEIR WEIGHT.

**BOOSTING EACH OTHER UP, RATHER THAN BRINGING EACH OTHER DOWN,** CAN CREATE A REALLY POSITIVE ENVIRONMENT, FULL OF ENERGY THAT IS SURE TO BOOST CONFIDENCE IN YOURSELF!

WHEN OTHERS SUPPORT YOU, IT IS AMAZING HOW MUCH MORE YOU FEEL YOU CAN SUPPORT YOURSELF. **UPLIFTING EACH OTHER AS WOMEN** CAN REALLY HELP TO BOOST CONFIDENCE AS A COLLECTIVE, AND TOGETHER WE CAN WORK TOWARDS A STRONGER, LOUDER AND MORE UNITED WORLD!

EMMELINE PANKHURST

JULY 15TH, 1858 – JUNE 14TH, 1928

MANCHESTER, ENGLAND.

## Founding member of the Suffragettes.

A BADASS FROM THE START, EMMELINE PANKHURST WAS INTRODUCED TO THE WOMEN'S SUFFRAGE MOVEMENT AT JUST AGE 14.

SHE SPENT HER ENTIRE LIFE ADVOCATING FOR WOMEN'S EQUALITY AND THEIR RIGHT TO VOTE. IN 1903, SHE FOUNDED THE WOMEN'S SOCIAL AND POLITICAL UNION (WSPU), A SUFFRAGE ORGANIZATION WHICH MADE THEIR VOICES HEARD IN A VERY LOUD WAY.

WITH FORCEFUL METHODS SUCH AS VANDALISM AND HUNGER STRIKES, THE ORGANIZATION HOPED TO SPREAD THE WORD THAT THEY WON'T STOP UNTIL WOMEN'S VOICES WERE HEARD LOUD AND CLEAR.

IN 1904, EMMELINE SYMPATHETICALLY PAUSED THE SUFFRAGE'S ACTIVITIES AND ENCOURAGED WOMEN TO SUPPORT BRITAIN IN THE FIRST WORLD WAR. INSPIRING THEM TAKE OVER MEN'S ROLES WITHIN THEIR COMMUNITIES WHILE THEY WERE AWAY FIGHTING, THIS SHOWED THE WORLD THAT WOMEN ARE STRONGER, BRAVER, AND MORE CAPABLE THAN THEY WERE PREVIOUSLY KNOWN TO BE!

## KATHRINE SWITZER

JANUARY 5TH, 1947

AMBERG, GERMANY.

# First woman to run the Boston Marathon.

ON APRIL 19TH, 1967, AT THE BOSTON MARATHON, KATHRINE SWITZER MADE HISTORY AS THE FIRST WOMAN TO SUCCESSFULLY ENTER AND RUN THE RACE.

SWITZER BEGAN TRAINING FOR IT AT SYRACUSE UNIVERSITY, AND DESPITE NOTHING IN THE RULE BOOK PROHIBITING WOMEN FROM ENTERING, IT WAS ASSUMED THAT NO WOMAN WOULD – KATHRINE WANTED TO BREAK THE MOLD!

AS SHE BEGAN RUNNING, OTHER MALE ENTRANTS WERE JEERING AND CONSTANTLY TRIED TO RUN HER OFF THE RACE. EVEN MORE FAMOUSLY, THE RACE'S ORGANIZER, JACK SEMPLE, KEPT ASSAULTING HER DURING THE RACE!

BUT FOR KATHRINE, THIS WAS ALL WATER OFF A DUCK'S BACK, AND SHE KNEW THAT SHE HAD TO CARRY ON TO MAKE HISTORY! FINISHING THE MARATHON IN 4 HOURS 20 MINUTES, SHE BECAME A CRUSADER FOR WOMEN'S SPORTS!

"My mother told me to be a
LADY.
And for her, that meant
be your own
person, be
INDEPENDENT."

- RUTH BADER GINSBURG

# Badass self-care

BEING A BADASS CAN BE TIRING WORK, AND EVEN THE MOST INSPIRING WOMEN ON EARTH NEED THEIR BEAUTY SLEEP.

PUTTING DOWN YOUR DEVICES, AVOIDING CAFFEINE, AND TAKING A BATH BEFORE BED ARE ALL BADASS WAYS TO HELP SLEEP COME EASIER TO YOU.

WHY NOT TAKE SOME TIME TO READ YOUR FAVOURITE BOOK, OR PRACTICE SOMETHING ENRICHING LIKE A HOBBY OR SELF-CARE RITUAL BEFORE BED? ALL OF THESE THINGS CAN SEND YOU INTO A DEEP SLEEP!

TRY TO GET AT LEAST 7-9 HOURS OF SLEEP A NIGHT - THIS WAY, YOU CAN FEEL REFRESHED, RECHARGE YOUR BATTERIES AND **BE READY TO TAKE ON THE WORLD IN YOUR OWN WAY!**

# MARY G. HARRIS JONES

AUGUST 1ST, 1837 – NOVEMBER 30TH, 1930
IRELAND (LIVED IN MARYLAND, USA).

## Fought for workers' rights and against child labor.

KNOWN AS 'MOTHER JONES', THIS DETERMINED HEROINE
FOUGHT FOR THE RIGHTS OF CHILD MILL WORKERS AND
INDUSTRIAL WORKERS, AND ORGANIZED MANY STRIKES
AND PROTESTS.

A BELOVED AND UNRELENTING ACTIVIST, MARY FIRST
WORKED AS A SCHOOLTEACHER AND THEN A SEAMSTRESS,
BUT IN 1867, A TRAGEDY STRUCK HER, AS HER ENTIRE
FAMILY DIED FROM YELLOW FEVER.

TEN YEARS LATER, MARY WAS DETERMINED TO HELP THE
WORKING POOR, FIGHTING FOR HIGHER WAGES, BETTER
WORKING ENVIRONMENTS, INSURANCE, AND HEALTHCARE.
ORGANIZING THE GREAT RAILROAD STRIKE OF 1877, MARY
LED HUNDREDS OF STRIKES AND RIOTS.

IN THE EARLY 1900'S, SHE FOCUSED ON PROTESTING FOR
MINERS, BUT AFTER A VIOLENT STRIKE IN WEST VIRGINIA,
SHE WAS CONVICTED OF CONSPIRACY TO COMMIT MURDER.

# HARRIET TUBMAN

MARCH, 1822 – MARCH 10TH, 1913
MARYLAND, USA.

## Escaped slavery and freed over 70 slaves.

HARRIET TUBMAN REALLY DOES BELONG IN THE BADASS HALL OF FAME! BORN INTO SLAVERY, THIS FIERCE WOMAN RAISED HER MIDDLE FINGER TO SLAVEHOLDERS IN THE 1800'S AND SAVED MANY LIVES IN THE PROCESS.

BEATEN AND WHIPPED AS A CHILD BY HER CAPTORS, HARRIET SUFFERED A BAD HEAD INJURY – LEAVING HER WITH HYPERSOMNIA, YET SHE DIDN'T GIVE IN, AND INSTEAD BEGAN PLANNING HER RISE TO FREEDOM!

IN 1849, SHE RISKED HER LIFE TO ESCAPE TO PHILADELPHIA (WHICH WAS A FREE STATE), AND FEARLESSLY RETURNED SOON AFTER TO FREE HER FAMILY. TRAVELLING IN SECRECY AT NIGHT, SHE CONTINUOUSLY WORKED TO HELP FREE AND GUIDE OTHER SLAVES AWAY FROM THEIR CAPTIVITY, AND FINDING THEM WORK IN CANADA.

MEETING ABOLITIONIST JOHN BROWN IN 1858, HARRIET HELPED HIM DEVISE A DARING PLAN AND RECRUITED SUPPORTERS FOR A RAID ON HARPERS FERRY. DURING THE CIVIL WAR, SHE BECAME A HARDCORE ARMED SCOUT AND SPY, LEADING AN ARMED EXPEDITION TO RAID COMBAHEE FERRY, LIBERATING OVER 700 SLAVES!

"IF YOU WANT
SOMETHING SAID,
*Ask a man;*
IF YOU WANT
SOMETHING DONE,
*Ask a woman.*"

- MARGARET THATCHER

# Everyone has natural gifts

**FIND YOURS AND RUN WITH IT!** REALLY FINDING YOUR GROOVE AND TALENTS CAN NOT ONLY MAKE YOUR PROFESSIONAL LIFE MUCH EASIER, IT WILL REALLY HELP YOU TO PROGRESS BY SIMPLY BEING YOURSELF!

WHETHER THAT IS SOMETHING INTELLECTUAL, CREATIVE OR PHYSICAL, PERSUING A CAREER PATH THAT ALLOWS YOU TO FLOURISH AND GROW THIS TALENT IS A GREAT WAY TO GIVE YOU A BADASS BOOST IN YOUR CHOSEN FIELD.

YOUR NATURAL GIFTS AND TALENTS ARE WHAT MAKES YOU WONDERFULLY UNIQUE, AND BY USING YOUR STRENGTHS, YOU CAN **PROVE TO THE WORLD WHAT A ONE-OF-A-KIND BOSS YOU REALLY ARE!**

AMANTINE LUCILE AURORE DUPIN

JULY 1ST, 1804 – JUNE 8TH, 1876

PARIS, FRANCE.

# Advocated for women and stood against female stereotypes.

AMANTINE LUCILE AURORE DUPIN DE FRANCUEIL, OTHERWISE KNOWN UNDER THE PEN NAME 'GEORGE SAND', WAS A FRENCH NOVELIST AND JOURNALIST WHO, QUITE FRANKLY, NEVER GAVE A SINGLE DAMN WHAT OTHER PEOPLE THOUGHT, AND STOOD STRONGLY AND LOUDLY AGAINST FEMALE STEREOTYPES!

WEARING MALE CLOTHES WITHOUT A PERMIT (WHICH WAS ILLEGAL), SMOKING TOBACCO IN PUBLIC, AND HER PROMISCUITY WERE ALL THINGS THAT WERE VERY FROWNED UPON, BUT SHE DIDN'T LET THAT STOP HER!

HER LOVERS INCLUDED COMPOSER FRÉDÉRIC CHOPIN, AND EVEN ACTRESS MARIE DORVAL, WHICH WAS HUGELY SCANDALOUS IN THE 19TH CENTURY!

SHE WAS ALSO A HUGE ADVOCATE FOR WOMEN'S RIGHTS, AND POOR AND WORKING CLASS COMMUNITIES IN HER WRITINGS, ALL OF WHICH WERE NOT POPULAR WITH MOST RESPECTED FIGURES OF HER TIME. THE BEST PART ABOUT HER? SHE JUST DIDN'T CARE!

# THE NIGHT WITCHES

YEARS ACTIVE: 1942–1945

RUSSIA.

## First all-female military aviators in WW2.

FORMED BY MAJOR MARINA RASKOVA, THE NIGHT WITCHES WERE THE FIRST EVER ALL-FEMALE AVIATION REGIMENT.

AT FIRST THEY WEREN'T WELCOMED KINDLY INTO THE MILITARY, AS THEY WERE SEEN AS INFERIOR TO THEIR MALE COMRADES, HOWEVER BY THE END OF THE WAR, THEY HAD ACHIEVED OVER 23,000 MISSIONS!

THE NIGHT WITCHES GOT THEIR NAME FROM THEIR GERMAN ENEMY, AS THEY WOULD IDLE THEIR PLANE ENGINES WHEN CLOSE TO THEIR TARGET, LEAVING NO OTHER NOISE EXCEPT A LOW WHISTLING FROM THE WIND.

THIRTY-TWO MEMBERS OF THE NIGHT WITCHES LOST THEIR LIVES DURING THE WAR, BUT THEIR SACRIFICE FOR THEIR COUNTRY INSPIRED MANY OTHER WOMEN TO JOIN THE MILITARY AND TAKE UP AVIATION!

"I RAISE UP MY

*Voice*

NOT SO I CAN
SHOUT BUT SO THAT
THOSE WITHOUT A VOICE
CAN BE HEARD...WE CANNOT
SUCCEED WHEN HALF
OF US ARE HELD BACK."

- MALALA YOUSAFZAI

# Take a breath

US WOMEN ARE KNOWN TO BE AMAZING MULTI-TASKERS, BUT SOMETIMES ALL THE THINGS WE HAVE GOING ON IN OUR LIVES CAN LEAVE US IN A MUDDLE... DON'T LET ALL YOUR THOUGHTS AND CHORES GET IN THE WAY OF BEING YOUR BEST SELF!

**A JOURNAL IS A GREAT WAY TO KEEP YOUR MIND CLEAR,** TASKS ORGANIZED, AND WILL HELP YOU JOT DOWN THINGS YOU MIGHT FORGET, SO YOU CAN SLAY THE DAY! EVEN IF YOU USE THIS JOURNAL TO JOT DOWN YOUR FEELINGS, EMOTIONS AND THOUGHTS THROUGHOUT THE DAY, ALONGSIDE YOUR TASKS - STAYING IN TUNE WITH HOW YOU ARE FEELING IS A GREAT WAY TO **STOP YOU GETTING OVERWHELMED BY DAILY LIFE!**

(FOR ADDED WELLBEING AND PEACE OF MIND, WHY NOT USE YOUR JOURNAL TO TRACK YOUR STEPS, WATER INTAKE, AND EVEN YOUR MONTHLY CYCLE?)

## MABEL CAPPER

JUNE 23RD, 1888 – SEPTEMBER 1ST, 1966
MANCHESTER, ENGLAND.

## Rebel Suffragette.

BORN INTO A FAMILY OF SUFFRAGETTES, IT'S NO WONDER
MABEL MADE HEADLINES IN HER WILD FIGHT AGAINST
SEXISM! HER MOTHER WAS A SUFFRAGETTE HERSELF, AND
HER FATHER BEING AN HONORARY SECRETARY FOR THE
MEN'S LEAGUE FOR WOMEN'S SUFFRAGE.

MABEL JOINED THE WSPU IN 1907 AT JUST AGE 19, AND
WAS IMPRISONED 6 TIMES – FOR ASSAULTING A CHIEF
INSPECTOR, VANDALISM, USING EXPLOSIVES, AND ARSON,
AMONG OTHER THINGS!

WHEN IMPRISONED, MABEL VOWED TO GO ON A HUNGER
STRIKE, AND THOUGH SHE WASN'T THE FIRST TO DO THIS,
SHE WAS THE FIRST SUFFRAGETTE TO BE FORCE-FED. THIS
CAUSED OUTRAGE, AND MANY SUFFRAGETTES TOOK A STAND
AGAINST THE POOR TREATMENT OF WOMEN IN PRISON.

WHEN THE SUFFRAGETTES WERE DISBANDED BECAUSE OF
THE FIRST WORLD WAR, MABEL JOINED THE VOLUNTEER AID
DETACHMENT TO HELP INJURED SOLDIERS.

IRENA SENDLER

FEBRUARY 15TH, 1910 – MAY 12TH, 2008

WARSAW, POLAND.

# Smuggled Jewish children out of Warsaw in World War Two.

GAINING SPECIAL PERMITS TO ENTER THE GHETTO, IRENA AND HER FRIEND BRAVELY SNUCK PAST NAZI SOLDIERS TO BRING MEDICATION TO THE WEAK, AND SNUCK IN FOOD, CLOTHING AND OTHER ITEMS TOO!

EVENTUALLY, IRENA AND HER FRIENDS RISKED CAPTURE BY SNEAKING OUT BABIES AND YOUNG CHILDREN, PLACING THEM WITH WILLING POLISH FAMILIES OR IN ORPHANAGES AND CONVENTS.

BETWEEN 1942 AND 1943, IRENA AND HER 10 COMPANIONS RELENTLESSLY SAVED 2,500 JEWISH CHILDREN. IRENA WAS SUDDENLY ARRESTED AND HER HOUSE TURNED UPSIDE DOWN FOR CLUES OF THE CHILDREN'S WHEREABOUTS. KNOWING THE FATE OF ALL 2,500 CHILDREN, SHE MANAGED TO PASS HER FRIEND JANINA THE LIST OF THE CHILDREN AND THEIR LOCATIONS.

IRENA REFUSED TO GIVE ANY INFORMATION TO THE ENEMY, AND WAS CONVICTED TO DEATH BY FIRING SQUAD. WHILE BEING TRANSPORTED HER TO HER DEATH, SHE ESCAPED WITH THANKS TO THE QUICK THINKING OF HER FRIEND MARIA!

"The success of every
WOMAN
should be the
INSPIRATION
to another.
We should raise
each other up."

— SERENA WILLIAMS

# Be proud

BE PROUD OF YOUR ACHIEVEMENTS! **GENDER DOES NOT DEFINE YOU,** BUT RECOGNIZE THE HARD WORK YOU HAVE PUT IN DESPITE THE SETBACKS YOU HAVE FACED!

**LOOK HOW MUCH YOU HAVE ACHIEVED IN YOUR CAREER** - 10 YEARS AGO, WOULD YOU HAVE THOUGHT YOU WOULD HAVE COME THIS FAR? EVEN IF IT IS THE LITTLE VICTORIES AND TASKS YOU COMPLETE EVERY DAY, BE PROUD OF MAKING IT THROUGH THEM AND OUT OF THE OTHER SIDE.

**CONTINUE TO RAISE THE BAR AND STRIVE TO DO YOUR BEST,** BUT EVEN IF SOMETIMES YOU FEEL DEFLATED, REMEMBER - YOU GOT THIS FAR! NOW THAT'S PRETTY BADASS!

# JEANNE DE CLISSON

1300 - 1359

BELLEVILLE, FRANCE.

## French aristocrat and pirate.

JEANNE DE CLISSON WAS A FRENCH NOBLEWOMAN – UNTIL HER HUSBAND WAS BEHEADED ON SUSPICION OF TREASON – AN EVENT THAT TURNED HER INTO ONE OF THE MOST DANGEROUS PIRATES IN THE ENGLISH CHANNEL!

DISTRAUGHT, SHE SOLD HER BELONGINGS TO RAISE ENOUGH MONEY TO CREATE HER FLEET, CALLED THE 'BLACK FLEET". SEEKING REVENGE, JEANNE DE CLISSON SAILED AROUND THE ENGLISH CHANNEL FOR 13 YEARS, AND GOT REVENGE FOR HER HUSBAND'S DEATH BY TARGETING FRENCH SHIPS THAT PASSED THROUGH THE CHANNEL.

THIS FORMER UNSUSPECTING NOBLEWOMAN QUICKLY BECAME A FEARED AND RUTHLESS FORCE, ESPECIALLY FOR FRENCH SAILORS. THAT'S WHAT HAPPENS WHEN YOU MAKE SOMEONE ANGRY ENOUGH!

JEANNE DE CLISSON WAS NEVER CAUGHT, AND ACTUALLY RETIRED BACK TO FRANCE (ONCE HER PIRACY DAYS WERE SATISFIED) WHERE SHE LIVED IN HENNEBONT CASTLE, UNTIL HER DEATH IN 1359!

# GRACE JONES

MAY 19TH, 1948

SPANISH TOWN, JAMAICA.

## Legendary musician and artist who bent boundaries around gender and sexuality.

GRACE JONES HAS ALWAYS BEEN A BADDIE THROUGHOUT HER CAREER IN MUSIC AND THE ARTS, PUSHING BOUNDARIES AND, FRANKLY, NOT GIVING A SINGLE DAMN WHAT ANYONE THOUGHT!

SINCE RELEASING MUSIC AND BEING IN THE PUBLIC EYE, GRACE JONES HAS EXPERIENCED MASS CRITICISM FOR HER SEXUALITY, FEMININITY AND GENDER EXPRESSION, BUT SHE NEVER LET THIS STOP HER FROM BEING TRUE TO HERSELF!

SHE DODGED BULLETS FIRED FROM THE MEDIA AND COMMENTS FROM MEN, AND PAVED THE WAY FOR WOMEN TO BE STRONG AND EXPRESSIVE, WHETHER THAT IS SEXUAL, MASCULINE OR FEMININE! WE HAVE HER TO THANK FOR A LOT OF OUR FAVORITE ARTISTS TODAY, AND THEIR FREEDOM TO DO WHAT THEY DO BEST.

ELLEN O'NEAL

C.1960 – OCTOBER 2020

SAN DIEGO, USA.

# A pioneer in women's skateboarding.

ELLEN O'NEAL GREW UP IN SAN DIEGO, AS A BALLET DANCER AND GYMNAST. SHE SOON FOUND A WAY TO COMBINE THESE SKILLS WITH HER PASSION FOR BODY SURFING BY SKATEBOARDING!

HER UNIQUE STYLE AND SKILLSET MEANT SHE QUICKLY DOMINATED THE FIELD, AND STOOD OUT IN A VERY MALE-DOMINATED SPORT! STARRING IN A 1967 FILM, 'SKATEBOARD', O'NEAL PROVED TO GIRLS THAT PASSION CAN TAKE YOU ANYWHERE, AND DESPITE THE DOUBTS OF OTHER PLAYERS AND ONLOOKERS, SHE WAS ABLE TO LEAVE HER MARK!

HER LOVE OF SKATEBOARDING, UNIQUE ROUTINES, AND DETERMINATION TO PAVE A WAY FOR WOMEN IN THE SPORT COMPLETELY CHANGED SKATEBOARDING FOREVER!

...COME ON – WHAT'S MORE BADASS THAN SKATEBOARDING?!

"A
STRONG
woman looks a
CHALLENGE
dead in the eye and
gives it a wink."

- GINA CAREY

# Find your cheerleaders

FIND YOUR CHEERLEADERS! THE PEOPLE IN YOUR LIFE WHO SUPPORT AND ADVOCATE FOR YOU.

IT'S IMPORTANT TO **SURROUND YOURSELF WITH GOOD PEOPLE** WHO NOT ONLY GIVE GOOD ADVICE BUT ALSO CHALLENGE YOU TO DO BETTER, AND ARE ALSO THERE FOR YOU WHEN THINGS MIGHT NOT GO YOUR WAY.

BADASS WOMEN SUPPORT OTHER BADASS WOMEN! THE POWER OF SISTERHOOD IS SO IMPORTANT, HELPING EACH OTHER PUT THE SUPPORT YOU WANT TO SEE FOR YOURSELF INTO THE WORLD!

# SAFFIYAH KHAN

NOVEMBER 27TH, 1997

BIRMINGHAM, ENGLAND.

## Smiled in the face of racial hatred.

WHAT'S THE BEST WAY TO ANNOY A RACIST? SMILE IN THEIR FACE – THIS IS EXACTLY WHAT SAFFIYAH KHAN DID!

IN 2017, TEENAGER SAFFIYAH KHAN FOUND HERSELF CAUGHT IN THE MIDDLE OF AN EDL (ENGLISH DEFENSE LEAGUE) RALLY IN BIRMINGHAM, UK.

STEPPING IN TO DEFEND A MUSLIM WOMAN WHO WAS UNDER ATTACK FROM THE MEMBERS OF THE RALLY, AND WHEN FACED WITH ONE OF THE ANGRY PROTESTERS, SHE SIMPLY SMILED! THIS IMAGE QUICKLY WENT VIRAL, AND SHOWED THE WORLD HOW FIGHTING HATRED WITH A SMILE IS A POWERFUL MESSAGE!

SAFFIYAH HAS SINCE GONE ON TO CAMPAIGN AND BE AN ACTIVIST FOR MANY CAUSES, SUCH AS FEMINISM AND RACIAL EQUALITY, AND USES HER VOICE AND PLATFORM TO SPEAK UP FOR PEOPLE WHO CAN'T!

# RUBY BRIDGES

SEPTEMBER 8TH, 1954

MISSISSIPPI, USA.

## Ended segregation by attending school.

SMALL BUT MIGHTY, RUBY BRIDGES WAS ONLY 6 YEARS OLD WHEN SHE SHOWED THE WORLD WHAT A BADASS SHE TRULY WAS!

AS THE FIRST PERSON TO DESEGREGATE THE ALL-WHITE WILLIAM FRANTZ ELEMENTARY SCHOOL IN 1960, RUBY FOUND HERSELF AT THE CENTER OF THE HATE AND OPPOSITION DESEGREGATION FACED!

WITH ONLY ONE TEACHER NOMINATING TO TEACH RUBY, AND EXPERIENCING CONSTANT HARASSMENT FROM OTHER FAMILIES, STUDENTS AND TEACHERS, INCLUDING DEATH THREATS AGAINST HER AND HER FAMILY, A YOUNG RUBY HELD HER HEAD HIGH AND PROVED TO LITTLE GIRLS EVERYWHERE THAT THERE IS HOPE FOR A MORE EQUAL FUTURE!

NOW, THIS YOUNG BADASS USES HER EXPERIENCE TO ADVOCATE AGAINST RACISM WITH HER OWN ORGANISATION 'THE RUBY BRIDGES FOUNDATION'.

ALEXANDRIA OCASIO-CORTEZ

OCTOBER 13TH, 1989

NEW YORK CITY, USA.

# Youngest woman ever elected into Congress.

ALEXANDRIA OCASIO-CORTEZ, COMMONLY KNOWN AS AOC, IS
AN AMERICAN POLITICIAN AND ACTIVIST. SHE BECAME NEW
YORK'S 14TH DISTRICT REPRESENTATIVE AT JUST 29 YEARS
OLD – MAKING HER THE YOUNGEST WOMAN TO EVER BE
ELECTED INTO CONGRESS!

STRIVING TO MAKE A CHANGE IN THE NEIGHBORHOOD SHE
GREW UP IN, AOC WAS ELECTED AS NEW YORK'S DISTRICT
REPRESENTATIVE IN CONGRESS IN 2018!

WHAT MAKES AOC A BADASS IS, DESPITE BEING YOUNG
AND LACKING RESPECT FROM MANY OTHER MEMBERS OF
CONGRESS, SHE WAS NOT AFRAID TO STAND AND FIGHT FOR
HER BELIEFS FROM DAY 1!

HER VERY FIRST SPEECH AS CONGRESSWOMAN
CONDEMNED PRESIDENT TRUMP AND HIS POLITICS,
AND CLEARLY OUTLINED THAT HER FIGHT TO UPLIFT
MINORITIES AND MARGINALIZED GROUPS IN NEW YORK,
AND ACROSS THE COUNTRY, WOULD NOT SLOW DOWN.

MORE POLITICIANS LIKE THIS, PLEASE?!

"Whatever
WOMEN
do, they must do twice
as well as men to be
thought half as good.
Luckily, this is not
DIFFICULT."

- CHARLOTTE WHITTON

# Everyone is different

ONE THING TO NOTE ABOUT THE BADASS WOMEN IN THIS BOOK, WHICH MAKES THEM INSPIRATIONAL AND AWE INDUCING, IS THAT THEY'RE ALL **UNIQUE!**

YOU DON'T NEED TO FIGHT AN ARMY OF MEN OR BREAK A WORLD RECORD TO MAKE SOMETHING OF YOURSELF, BUT YOU SHOULD KEEP IN MIND THAT **EVERYONE IS DIFFERENT, AND YOUR STRENGTHS ARE JUST AS UNIQUE AS YOURSELF.**

HAVING CONFIDENCE IN YOUR INDIVIDUAL STRENGTH AND DETERMINATION WILL HELP YOU **USE YOUR SKILLSET TO HELP OTHERS** AND **PUSH YOURSELF TO SUCCEED** IN YOUR OWN GOALS AND ASPIRATIONS!

# ROSE MCGOWAN

SEPTEMBER 5TH, 1973

FLORENCE, ITALY.

## One of the first women to speak up against Harvey Weinstein.

ACTRESS ROSE MCGOWAN FAMOUSLY WENT HEAD TO HEAD WITH HARVEY WEINSTEIN, AND BRAVELY MADE SURE HE ENDED UP BEHIND BARS!

IN 2016, MCGOWAN CAME FORWARD AND SPOKE UP ABOUT THE ABUSE BOTH HERSELF AND COUNTLESS OTHERS SUFFERED BY WEINSTEIN, AND STOOD STRONG AND UNITED WITH OTHER WOMEN TO GET JUSTICE!

HARVEY WEINSTEIN WAS AN EXTREMELY POWERFUL FIGURE IN HOLLYWOOD, AND ROSE MCGOWAN PUT HER WHOLE CAREER AND REPUTATION ON THE LINE TO VOICE WHAT MANY OTHERS WERE TOO SCARED TO SAY.

HER BRAVERY LED TO HIS ARREST, AND ALSO INSPIRED THE 'METOO' CAMPAIGN, THAT HELPED WOMEN STAND TOGETHER AGAINST ASSAULT ALL OVER THE WORLD!

ANDRÉE RAYMONDE BORREL

NOVEMBER 18TH, 1919 – JULY 6TH, 1944
PARIS, FRANCE.

# Helped airmen escape the Nazis.

THIS FEARLESS FRENCH BADASS GAVE A KICK TO THE BALLS OF ALL NAZIS, WITH HER BRAVE EFFORTS TO SAVE AS MANY SOLDIERS AS SHE COULD!

IN WORLD WAR TWO, ANDRÉE BORREL BECAME A PART OF THE SECRET UNDERGROUND ORGANIZATION, THE PAT O'LEARY LINE, HELPING STRANDED SOLDIERS AND AIRMEN ESCAPE NAZI CAPTURE.

ONCE THE ORGANIZATION DISBANDED, ANDRÉE TRAINED TO BECOME A FIELD AGENT. UNDER CODENAME 'DENISE', ANDRÉE BECAME ONE OF THE FIRST SOE WOMEN TO PARACHUTE INTO OCCUPIED FRANCE, AND PARTICIPATED IN DANGEROUS ESPIONAGE MISSIONS!

CAUGHT BY GERMAN SOLDIERS IN 1943, ANDRÉE AND OTHERS WERE ARRESTED, BEATEN, AND MOVED TO GERMANY IN 1944, WHERE THEY WERE EXECUTED.

A BADASS TO THE VERY END, ANDRÉE IS AN INSPIRATION TO ALL WOMEN, TO NEVER GIVE UP ON WHAT YOU BELIEVE IN!

# TOMOE GOZEN

## 12TH CENTURY

## JAPAN.

# Commanding Warrior in the late 12th century.

A FEARLESS WARRIOR WITH A SWORD, TOMOE GOZEN WAS A RELENTLESS FEMALE LEADER IN THE WORLD OF MEN.

THOUGH NOT UNCOMMON FOR WOMEN TO BE SKILLED IN MARTIAL ARTS, TOMOE GOZEN IS WELL KNOWN FOR BRAVELY COMMANDING AN ARMY OF 300 FEMALE SAMURAI UNDER THE LEADERSHIP OF YOSHINAKA, INTO BATTLE AGAINST 2,000 WARRIORS FROM THEIR RIVAL, THE TAIRA CLAN.

THOUGH ONLY ONE OF FIVE WARRIORS TO SURVIVE, TOMOE DIDN'T BACK DOWN, AND TWO YEARS LATER, SHE COMMANDED YET ANOTHER ARMY OF 3,000 MEN ALONGSIDE YOSHINAKA INTO THE BATTLE OF AWAZU.

THOUGH THE ARMY BECAME OUTNUMBERED AND SAW THE FALL OF YOSHINAKA, TOMOE WOULD BE AN INSPIRATION FOR FEMALE SAMURAI FOR CENTURIES TO COME.

"IF YOU DON'T LIKE THE ROAD YOU'RE WALKING *Start Paving* ANOTHER ONE."

- DOLLY PARTON

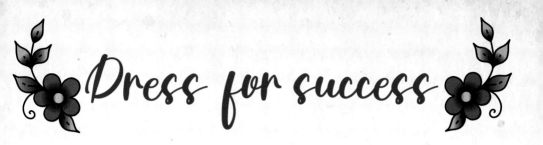

# Dress for success

BADASS WOMEN THROUGH THE YEARS HAVE TIRELESSLY BROKEN DOWN THE HARMFUL STEREOTYPES OF HOW A WOMAN AT WORK SHOULD APPEAR.

**THE RULE BOOK IS TORN UP** AND THE MAIN LESSON HERE IS TO **WEAR WHAT MAKES YOU FEEL CONFIDENT** – WHETHER THAT'S A BRIGHTER SHADE OF LIPSTICK OR A BOLD PRINT.

ALLOW YOUR PERSONAL WEEKEND STYLE TO INFLUENCE AND ADAPT YOUR WORK WARDROBE – DON'T HIDE AWAY YOUR PERSONALITY FROM THE OFFICE – IT'S WHAT MAKES YOU, YOU!

SIMPLE CHANGES TO YOUR POSTURE CAN ALSO HELP TO FORCE THIS INNER SELF-ASSURANCE – MAKE SURE YOU HOLD YOUR SHOULDERS BACK – THIS WILL HELP TO MAKE YOU LOOK TALLER AND BRIGHTER WHEN YOU WALK INTO THE ROOM.

**WHEN YOU ENTER A ROOM WITH YOUR HEAD HELD HIGH, PEOPLE WILL STOP AND LISTEN.** IN THE WORDS OF MARILYN MONROE –

## "Give a girl the right shoes and she can conquer the world."!

# SIMONE SEGOUIN

OCTOBER 3RD, 1925 – FEBRUARY 21ST, 2023
THIVARS, FRANCE.

## Teenage French Resistance Fighter.

STARTING OFF SMALL, THIS TEENAGE TROOPER BECAME A
FEARLESS RESISTANCE FIGHTER IN THE SECOND WORLD WAR!

SIMONE SEGOUIN WAS THE DAUGHTER OF A DECORATED
SOLDIER WHO FOUGHT IN THE FIRST WORLD WAR, AND
INSPIRED HER TO RISE TO THE CHALLENGE WHEN THE SECOND
WAR ERUPTED.

AT JUST AGE 17, SIMONE MET LIEUTENANT ROLAND
BOURSIER, WHO SPARKED HER INTEREST IN THE RESISTANCE.
THE LIEUTENANT INSTRUCTED SIMONE IN THE PROPER USE
OF SUBMACHINE GUNS, RIFLES AND HANDGUNS. FAKING
DOCUMENTS NEEDED, SHE MANAGED TO FAKE HER WAY INTO
THE COMMUNIST RESISTANCE FORCES (FTP), UNDER THE
ALIAS NICOLE MINET.

SHE BEGAN BY STEALING A BICYCLE FROM A GERMAN
PATROL, USING IT TO CARRY MESSAGES AND WEAPONS,
AND AS TIME WENT ON, THE JOBS SHE HAD TO DO BECAME
TOUGHER AND MORE DANGEROUS. CAPTURING GERMAN
TROOPS, SABOTAGING NAZI MISSIONS AND DERAILING ENEMY
TRAINS WERE JUST SOME ACTS OF RESISTANCE SIMONE
PARTICIPATED IN. BY THE AGE OF 18, SIMONE HAD ALREADY
ENABLED THE ARREST OF 25 GERMAN SOLDIERS!

# ROSA PARKS

FEBRUARY 4TH, 1913 – OCTOBER 24TH, 2005

ALABAMA, USA.

## Stood against racial segregation.

THE BADASS ON THE BUS, ROSA PARKS, WOULD MAKE A STAND FOR EQUALITY THAT WOULD SHAKE THE WORLD AND INSPIRE MANY OTHERS TO FOLLOW IN HER FOOTSTEPS!

IN THE 1950'S, MANY PUBLIC AREAS WERE SEGREGATED BY RACE, AND THE SAME WAS TRUE FOR BUSSES. ROSA REBELLIOUSLY REJECTED A BUS DRIVER'S ORDER TO MOVE FROM HER SEAT TO ALLOW A WHITE PASSENGER TO SIT DOWN, WHICH CAUSED AN OUTRAGE AND RESULTED IN HER BEING ARRESTED AND FOUND GUILTY OF DISORDERLY CONDUCT.

THOUGH NOT THE FIRST TO STAND HER GROUND ON A BUS, ROSA'S DEFIANCE OF THE INHUMANE LAW AND THE COURT CASE THAT FOLLOWED INSPIRED A NEWCOMER TO THE TOWN, MARTIN LUTHER KING JR., TO ARRANGE A BOYCOTT OF THE CITY'S BUSSES. MANY PEOPLE CARPOOLED AND WALKED FOR MILES INSTEAD OF USING PUBLIC TRANSPORT, TO PUNISH THE TRANSPORTATION COMPANY FOR THEIR TERRIBLE ACTIONS.

"Sometimes an ANGEL, sometimes a HELL-RAISER, always a STRONG WOMAN."

- R.H. SIN

# Inspire yourself

YES, **INSPIRATION** IS ALL AROUND YOU, AND THE WORLD IS FILLED WITH BRILLIANT AND AWE-INSPIRING PEOPLE WHO HAVE ACHIEVED GREAT THINGS!

OTHER PEOPLE'S STRENGTH, COURAGE, CREATIVITY, INTELLECT AND ACHIEVEMENTS COULD ALL BE A SOURCE OF INSPIRATION FOR YOU. **BUT WHO SAYS YOU CANNOT INSPIRE YOURSELF?**

YOU ARE BEAUTIFULLY UNIQUE IN YOUR OWN WAY, AND BY PLACING VALUE IN YOUR OWN ACHIEVEMENTS, AND BELIEVING IN YOUR OWN FUTURE (JUST AS THESE AMAZING WOMEN HAVE DONE FOR THEMSELVES) IS A GREAT WAY TO GIVE YOURSELF A BOOST!

SPEAK YOUR TRUTH, FOLLOW YOUR PASSIONS, AND FOCUS ON ENJOYING YOUR LIFE THE WAY YOU WANT TO! INSTEAD OF FOLLOWING FOOTSTEPS, WALK ALONGSIDE THEM! **BEING UNAPOLOGETICALLY YOURSELF AND USING YOUR OWN PASSIONS AND INTERESTS AS INSPIRATION** WILL EMPOWER YOU TO BE THE BADASS YOU WERE ALWAYS BORN TO BE!

# TESS ASPLUND

1974

CALI, COLOMBIA.

## Faced off against 300 Neo-Nazis.

WHAT DO YOU CALL A WOMAN WHO SINGLEHANDEDLY STANDS UP AGAINST 300 NEO-NAZIS? A TOTAL BADASS!

ORIGINALLY FROM COLOMBIA, COURAGEOUS TESS ASPLUND MOVED TO SWEDEN. BEING MIXED RACE, SHE QUICKLY FOUND THAT SHE WOULD FACE DISCRIMINATION AND HARASSMENT DUE TO THE COLOR OF HER SKIN.

THIS DIDN'T STOP HER. TESS BECAME AN ENTHUSIASTIC SWEDISH ACTIVIST, CAMPAIGNING FOR EQUALITY AND FOUGHT AGAINST NEO-NAZIS, BRAVELY BATTLING INTIMIDATING AND THREATENING GROUPS.

SHE GAINED ATTENTION FOLLOWING A STRIKING VIRAL IMAGE OF HER PROTESTING ALONE AGAINST ANGERED NEO-NAZIS IN BORLÄNGE, SWEDEN. TAKEN IN 2016, TESS CAN BE SEEN RAISING HER FIST IN THE AIR, AS SHE COMES FACE-TO-FACE WITH A CROWD OF OVER 300 NEO-NAZIS. SHE DOESN'T EVEN BREAK A SWEAT – PRETTY BADASS!

*"I was thinking: hell no, they can't march here! I had this adrenaline. No Nazi is going to march here, it's not okay." – Tess Asplund, May 4th, 2016*

"I AM NOT
*Free*
WHILE ANY WOMAN
*Is Unfree*
EVEN WHEN HER SHACKLES
ARE VERY DIFFERENT
FROM MY OWN."

- AUDRE LORDE

# Embrace your failures

THINGS DON'T ALWAYS GO TO PLAN, BUT THAT'S OKAY! YOU MIGHT FIND FAILURE FRUSTRATING AND OFF-PUTTING, BUT IF THE BADASS WOMEN IN THIS BOOK GAVE UP THEIR DREAMS AND PASSIONS AT THEIR FIRST OBSTACLE, THEY'D BE  UNHEARD OF.

DON'T LET MISTAKES OR FAILED ATTEMPTS KNOCK YOUR **CONFIDENCE** IN YOURSELF, MORE OFTEN THAN NOT, IT TAKES MORE THAN ONE ATTEMPT TO SUCCEED.

**YOU DON'T HAVE TO LIKE FAILURE, BUT YOU SHOULD EMBRACE IT.** FIND OUT WHERE YOU WENT WRONG, LEARN HOW TO MAKE IT RIGHT AND GROW FROM THE EXPERIENCE.

USE YOUR FAILURE TO STRIVE FOR GREATNESS!

# RONDA ROUSEY

**FEBRUARY 1ST, 1987**

**CALIFORNIA, USA.**

## Professional wrestler and UFC fighter.

PROFESSIONAL WRESTLER AND MIXED MARTIAL ARTIST RONDA ROUSEY MAY SEEM JUST LIKE ANY OTHER FIGHTER – HOWEVER SHE IS FAR MORE!

HER BEAUTIFUL, HARD OUTER SHELL HAS BECOME ONE OF THE MOST RECOGNIZABLE FACES IN UFC HISTORY, PAVING THE WAY FOR WOMEN TO COMPETE!

IN 2008, ROUSEY COMPETED IN THE 2008 BEIJING OLYMPIC GAMES IN WOMEN'S JUDO, AND BECAME THE FIRST AMERICAN TO WIN AN OLYMPIC MEDAL IN THE SPORT. SINCE THEN, ROUSEY HAS GONE FROM STRENGTH TO STRENGTH.

TRAINED IN MMA FIGHTING, ROUSEY WISHED TO PURSUE UFC, WHICH AT THE TIME HAD BEEN A MALE-ONLY SPORT SINCE ITS ORIGINS 20 YEARS PREVIOUSLY. APPLYING PRESSURE TO THE UFC BOARD, IN 2012 SHE BECAME THE FIRST FEMALE FIGHTER TO SIGN WITH THEM, AND PROCEEDED TO BE UNDEFEATED FOR 3 YEARS!

NOW A WRESTLER FOR WWE, AND AFTER BEING INDUCTED INTO THE UFC HALL OF FAME, ROUSEY IS HAILED AS A TRAILBLAZER FOR WOMEN IN MALE-DOMINATED SPORTS!

# BOUDICCA

30 AD (EST) - 61 AD.

## Queen of the Iceni tribe.

BOUDICCA WAS AN ANCIENT QUEEN OF THE BRITISH ICENI TRIBE, WHO IS FAMED FOR LEADING AN ARMY AGAINST THE ROMANS IN 60 AD. GOING AGAINST AN ARMY AS POWERFUL AS THE ROMAN EMPIRE'S, SHE IS REMEMBERED FOR HER STRENGTH, BRAVERY, AND FOR BEING A STRAIGHT UP BADASS WARRIOR!

BEFORE THE LEGENDARY BATTLE, BOUDICCA TRIED TO COME TO A DIPLOMATIC RESOLUTION WITH THE ROMANS, BUT THEIR MISOGYNY MEANT THEY HAD NO RESPECT FOR HER AS A LEADER, AND SO THE ONLY WAY TO PROVE HER STRENGTH WOULD BE TO GO TO BATTLE.

OVERRUNNING TOWNS, TEARING DOWN TEMPLES AND STRIKING FEAR INTO THE ROMANS, BOUDICCA PROVED THAT WOMEN CAN BE EQUALLY FIERCE WARRIORS, AND DEMANDED RESPECT!

DESPITE THE CELTS LOSING IN THEIR FINAL BATTLE IN ANCIENT LONDINIUM, BOUDICCA HAD FINALLY WON SOMETHING — THE RESPECT OF THE ROMAN EMPIRE!

ALTHEA NEALE GIBSON

AUGUST 25TH, 1927 – SEPTEMBER 28TH, 2003

SOUTH CAROLINA, USA.

# One of the first athletes to fight color segregation.

ALTHEA GIBSON WAS A PROFESSIONAL GOLFER AND TENNIS PLAYER, BUT IS WIDELY KNOWN FOR HER WORK FIGHTING RACIAL SEGREGATION IN SPORT.

AS A CHILD, SHE PRACTICED PLAYING PADDLE TENNIS, AND BY THE AGE OF 12, SHE WAS THE CHAMPION IN NEW YORK CITY'S WOMEN'S PADDLE TENNIS.

HOWEVER, DESPITE HER RISING FAME, ALTHEA WAS BANNED FROM ENTERING THE UNITED STATES NATIONAL CHAMPIONSHIPS, AS SHE WAS UNABLE TO ACCUMULATE ENOUGH POINTS, WITH THE SANCTIONED TOURNAMENTS BEING HELD AT "WHITE-ONLY" CLUBS.

AFTER FIGHTING AGAINST THE RACISM WITH THE HELP OF RETIRED CHAMPION ALICE MARBLE, ALTHEA WAS INVITED TO THE NATIONALS. ALTHEA THEN WENT ON TO BECOME THE FIRST AFRICAN AMERICAN TO WIN A GRAND SLAM TITLE, AND EVEN INSPIRED VENUS AND SERENA WILLIAMS TO FOLLOW IN HER FOOTSTEPS!

## CHING SHIH

1775 - 1844

GUANGDONG PROVINCE, CHINA.

## Chinese Pirate Leader.

WHEN SOMEONE HAS ADOPTED THE NICKNAME 'CHINA'S PIRATE QUEEN', IT IS PRETTY CLEAR THAT BEING CALLED AN ABSOLUTE BADASS IS WARRANTED!

LIVING THROUGH THE QING DYNASTY, FORMER PROSTITUTE CHING SHIH WED TO CHENG I, WHO WAS A FAMOUS AND FEARSOME PIRATE. ON HIS DEATH, SHE FOUND HERSELF STEPPING INTO HER HUSBAND'S SHOES, AND COMMANDED 1,800 PIRATE SHIPS AND 80,000 MEN!

THIS MEANS THAT CHING SHIH'S FLEET, CALLED THE RED FLAG FLEET, REMAINS THE LARGEST IN HISTORY – TO WHICH SHE EVEN HAS A GUINNESS WORLD RECORD!

TO GAIN CONTROL OF HER PIRATES, SHE ESTABLISHED STRICT LAWS, WHICH ALSO STOOD TO EMPOWER THE SMALL NUMBER OF WOMEN WHO WERE ALSO LIVING ON THE SHIPS.

UNDER HER RULE, THE RED FLAG FLEET WERE UNDEFEATED, DESPITE MANY ATTEMPTS TO CONQUER IT. CHING FINALLY RETIRED BY ACCEPTING AN OFFER OF AMNESTY FROM CHINA'S GOVERNMENT IN 1810, AND LIVED FOR A FURTHER 34 YEARS!

SHE IS NOW KNOWN AS ONE OF THE MOST PROLIFIC AND SUCCESSFUL PIRATES IN HISTORY, AND JUST GOES TO SHOW THAT WHATEVER MEN CAN DO, WOMEN CAN DO BETTER!

"BE THE KIND OF

*Woman*

WHO, WHEN YOUR FEET HIT
THE FLOOR EACH MORNING,
THE DEVIL SAYS,

"*Oh, no! She's up.*"

- JOANNE CLANCY

# Focus on the positives

SOMETHING ALL OF THESE BADASS WOMEN HAVE IN COMMON, IS THEY WERE HEADSTRONG AND DETERMINED TO FOLLOW THROUGH WITH WHAT THEY WANT OUT OF LIFE!

TO FEED THIS INTO YOUR GENERAL WELL-BEING, TRY TO **THINK ABOUT WHAT YOU WANT FROM LIFE, RATHER THAN WHAT YOU DON'T WANT.**

CHANGING THIS NARRATIVE IN YOUR APPROACH IS A GREAT WAY TO COMPLETELY CHANGE YOUR OUTLOOK – IT'S AMAZING HOW A POSITIVE VIEW ON YOUR GOALS BRINGS EVERYTHING WITHIN REACH.

DON'T THINK ABOUT WHAT YOU CAN'T DO, BUT FOCUS ON WHAT YOU CAN! INSTEAD OF THINKING ABOUT (AND FOCUSING ON) YOUR SETBACKS, CONSIDER THINKING ABOUT THE OPPORTUNITIES YOU CAN CREATE FOR YOURSELF, THE INSPIRATION THAT IS ALL AROUND YOU, AND **THE PATH YOU WANT TO CARVE OUT FOR YOURSELF!**

THIS WILL DO WONDERS FOR YOUR GENERAL OUTLOOK ON LIFE – BECAUSE **WHAT YOU SEEK, YOU WILL FIND!**

MARCH 25TH, 1942 – AUGUST 16TH, 2018

MEMPHIS, TENNESSEE, USA.

# The Queen of Soul, and the first woman in the Rock and Roll hall of fame.

LEGENDARY SINGER, SONGWRITER AND PIANIST, ARETHA FRANKLIN, CARVED HER OWN PATH IN THE MUSIC INDUSTRY AND PIONEERED THE WAY FOR WOMEN IN SOUL AND ROCK MUSIC!

RECORDING HER FIRST ALBUM, THE GOSPEL SOUND OF ARETHA FRANKLIN WHEN SHE WAS ONLY 14 YEARS OLD, SHE SOON BECAME ONE OF THE GREATEST SINGERS THAT HAS EVER LIVED, AND HAS EVEN LANDED IN THE TOP SPOT OF ROLLING STONE'S 100 GREATEST SINGERS OF ALL TIME!

HER MUSIC TOUCHED THE ENTIRE WORLD, BUT WAS MASSIVELY IMPORTANT FOR AFRICAN AMERICAN WOMEN IN AMERICA, AS SHE DEMANDED RESPECT AND PROVED THAT WOMEN, ESPECIALLY WOMEN OF COLOR, COULD BE STRONG, INDEPENDENT, VOCAL AND SUCCESSFUL!

EARNING THE TITLE 'THE QUEEN OF SOUL', AND BEING THE FIRST WOMAN EVER TO BE ADOPTED INTO THE ROCK AND ROLL HALL OF FAME IN 1987, ARETHA'S SELF-TAUGHT CAREER HAS PROVED THAT AGAINST THE ODDS, WITH TALENT AND DETERMINATION, YOU CAN CARVE OUT YOUR OWN AWESOME LEGACY!

# JOAN OF ARC

1412 – MAY 30TH, 1431

VOSGES, FRANCE.

## Led the French army to victory.

SAID TO HAVE BEEN GUIDED BY VISIONS OF ARCHANGEL MICHAEL, SAINT MARGARET, AND SAINT CATHERINE, JOAN BELIEVED SHE WAS A PROPHET, CHOSEN TO SAVE FRANCE FROM DOMINATION OF THEIR ENEMIES.

AT ONLY 17 YEARS OLD, JOAN BRAVELY BECAME A MEMBER OF A RELIEF ARMY, UNDER THE ORDER OF KING CHARLES VII. SHE WIELDED A FRENCH BANNER AND BROUGHT HOPE TO THE FRENCH SOLDIERS. AFTER FRANCE'S VICTORY, JOAN WAS CELEBRATED HIGHLY ACROSS THE COUNTRY, AND WAS INVOLVED IN MANY MORE SIEGES.

CAPTURED BY BURGUNDIANS, AN ALLY OF ENGLAND, JOAN WAS PUT ON TRIAL BY BISHOP PIERRE CAUCHON FOR WITCHCRAFT, HEARSY, ACTING UPON DEMONIC VISIONS, AND BLASPHEMY BY WEARING MALE CLOTHING. DECLARED GUILTY, SHE WAS BURNED AT THE STAKE AT AGE 19.

SADLY TOO LATE FOR JOAN, IN 1456 THE VERDICT WAS OVERTURNED, AND JOAN WAS REVERED AS A MARTYR, AND BECAME A PATRON SAINT FOR FRANCE.

# "I AM A

# *Woman*

# AND WHEN I THINK,
# I MUST

# *Speak.*"

- BEYONCÉ

# Fight for what's right

DEVELOPING A CAUSE OR A PURPOSE TO DRIVE YOU IS A GREAT WAY TO GIVE YOU A SENSE OF GROUNDING AND COMMUNITY, WHICH IS GREAT FOR YOUR MENTAL WELL-BEING!

SOMETHING AS SMALL AS VOLUNTEERING OR CAMPAIGNING FOR LOCAL CHARITIES AND CAUSES, TO FINDING A SPECIAL CAUSE YOU ARE PASSIONATE ABOUT, OR EVEN JOINING GROUPS OF LIKE-MINDED INDIVIDUALS CAN REALLY HELP YOU BRING A SENSE OF FOCUS, DRIVE AND COMMUNITY TO YOUR INTERESTS AND PASSIONS!

THE ABILITY TO HELP OTHERS AND JOIN FORCES TO SELFLESSLY HELP THOSE LESS FORTUNATE THAN YOURSELF CAN ALSO BRING FORWARD PRIDE IN YOUR ACTIONS, AND **HIGHLIGHT THE POWER YOU HOLD IN CHANGING THE WORLD** IN YOUR ACTIONS – HOWEVER SMALL OR BIG!

**TO HELP OTHERS CAN ALSO HELP YOURSELF!**

# SYLVIA RIVERA

JULY 2ND, 1951 – FEBRUARY 19, 2002
NEW YORK CITY, USA.

## A powerful activist in the American gay and transgender liberation movement.

SYLVIA RIVERA, WHO'S GENDER WAS ASSIGNED MALE AT BIRTH, HAD AN EXTREMELY DIFFICULT UPBRINGING, BUT DIDN'T LET THIS STOP HER FROM FIGHTING FOR MORE POWER TO MARGINALIZED GROUPS!

RUNNING AWAY FROM HOME AT THE AGE OF 11, SYLVIA MET ACTIVIST MARSHA P. JOHNSON AT AGE 13, WHO INSPIRED HER TO FIGHT AND STAND UP FOR HERSELF!

SYLVIA'S ACTIVISM LED TO HER INVOLVEMENT WITH THE STONEWALL UPRISING, WHICH BECAME A TURNING POINT OF THE ENTIRE GAY RIGHTS MOVEMENT IN THE USA!

SYLVIA WAS ALWAYS VICIOUSLY HERSELF, FOUGHT FOR PEOPLE WHO COULDN'T FIGHT FOR THEMSELVES, AND DIDN'T LET EVEN EXTREME SETBACKS SQUASH HER SPIRIT OR PRIDE – NOW THAT'S A BADASS!

# ALICE HUYLER RAMSEY

## NOVEMBER 11TH, 1886 – SEPTEMBER 10TH, 1983
### NEW JERSEY, USA

## First woman to drive an automobile across the USA.

ALICE RAMSEY WAS THE FIRST WOMAN TO DRIVE AN AUTOMOBILE ACROSS THE UNITED STATES, WHICH ALSO MADE HER THE FIRST WOMAN TO BE INDUCTED INTO THE AUTOMOTIVE HALL OF FAME!

AT ONLY 22, SHE WAS ALREADY AN EXPERIENCED DRIVER, AND WANTING TO FIGHT FOR A WOMAN'S RIGHT TO DRIVE FREELY, SET OFF WITH THREE OF HER FRIENDS ON A JOURNEY OF A LIFETIME!

BEING THE ONLY WOMAN IN THE VEHICLE WHO COULD DRIVE, THE GROUP CAME ACROSS MANY DIFFICULT CHALLENGES; 11 FLAT TIRES, BAD ROAD SURFACES, HARSH WEATHER AND BREAKDOWNS.

IN NEBRASKA, THE WOMEN ENCOUNTERED ARMED NATIVE AMERICANS, WHO DESPITE THEIR FIERCE APPEARANCES, TREATED THE WOMEN KINDLY.

IN WYOMING, THEIR VEHICLE BECAME SURROUNDED BY A POSSE ON HORSEBACK – WHO WERE LOOKING FOR A MURDERER ON THE RUN. THE POSSE DIDN'T BELIEVE THE BRAVE WOMEN'S STORY ABOUT THEIR JOURNEY, AND SEARCHED THE VEHICLE.

AFTER 59 DAYS, THE WOMEN CROSSED OVER TO OAKLAND BAY – SUCCEEDING IN THEIR MISSION TO TRAVEL THE USA!

# "THE MOST ALLURING THING A WOMAN CAN HAVE IS

## *Confidence.* "

- BEYONCÉ

# Talk to yourself

TALKING TO YOURSELF THROUGH THE MIRROR MIGHT
SOUND LIKE AN EMBARRASSING THING TO DO, BUT
**GIVING YOURSELF PEP-TALKS CAN ACTUALLY HELP
BOOST YOUR CONFIDENCE.**

BEING COMFORTABLE TO TALK TO YOURSELF OUT LOUD
IS A SKILL THAT CAN HELP YOUR SOCIAL INTERACTIONS
AND STAGE-FRIGHT, AND CAN EVEN RALLY YOU UP
AND EASE NERVES WHEN DOING SOMETHING NEW AND
DARING!

(HOW ELSE WILL YOU STAND UP FOR THE THINGS YOU
BELIEVE IN?)

# PUSSY RIOT

RUSSIA.

## Fighting and protesting for women's and LGBTQIA+ rights in Russia.

PUSSY RIOT ARE A RUSSIAN FEMINIST PUNK GROUP THAT PUBLICLY AND FEARLESSLY STAND UP FOR FEMINISM AND LGBTQIA+ RIGHTS IN THEIR PERFORMANCES. THEY WANT TO DRAW ATTENTION TO THE OPPRESSION IN PUTIN'S RUSSIA!

THEY WERE FOUNDED IN AUGUST 2011, AND SHOT TO FAME AFTER THEIR ANTI-PUTIN PERFORMANCE AT THE ALTAR IN ST BASIL'S CATHEDRAL IN MOSCOW, RUSSIA. AFTER THIS, TWO MEMBERS WERE JAILED FOR 21 MONTHS!

THEY CONTINUE TO FIGHT FOR THE RIGHTS OF RUSSIA'S WOMEN AND LGBTQIA+ MEMBERS, AND ARE NOT SCARED OR ASHAMED TO TAKE ON ONE OF THE WORLD'S MOST POWERFUL MEN!

# MARGARET SANGER

SEPTEMBER 14TH, 1879 – SEPTEMBER 6TH, 1966

NEW YORK, USA.

## Opened first U.S. birth control clinic.

AS A BIRTH-CONTROL ACTIVIST, SEX EDUCATOR, AND NURSE, MARGARET FOUGHT HARD TO POPULARIZE BIRTH CONTROL, IN ORDER TO GIVE WOMEN THE RIGHT TO DENY PREGNANCY AND REDUCE BACK-ALLEY ABORTIONS, SINCE ABORTION WAS ILLEGAL THROUGHOUT THE U.S.

IN 1916, MARGARET OPENED UP THE FIRST BIRTH CONTROL CLINIC IN THE U.S., IMPORTING DIAPHRAGMS ILLEGALLY FROM EUROPE, AS THESE WERE ONE OF THE MOST EFFECTIVE FORMS OF CONTRACEPTION AT THE TIME. THE CLINIC WAS SEEN AS TABOO AND WAS FROWNED UPON BY MANY, AND JUST NINE DAYS AFTER ITS OPENING, MARGARET WAS ARRESTED AND FORCED TO PAY $500 BAIL.

CONTINUING TO TREAT AND ADVISE WOMEN WHILE ON BAIL, MARGARET AND HER SISTER ETHEL WERE ARRESTED ONCE AGAIN, BOTH BEING SENTENCED TO 30 DAYS IN A WORKHOUSE, IN WHICH SHE TOLD THE COURT "I CANNOT RESPECT THE LAW AS IT EXISTS TODAY".

THE ARREST CREATED AN UPROAR WHICH INSPIRED OTHERS TO PROTEST, AND IN 1918, THE BIRTH CONTROL MOVEMENT WON A VICTORY, AS A RULING WAS PUT IN PLACE TO ALLOW CONTRACEPTIVES TO BE ISSUED BY DOCTORS.

"Only she who
ATTEMPTS
the absurd can
ACHIEVE
the impossible."

- ROBIN MORGAN

# Ditch the doubt

ONE THING ALL OUR BADASS WOMEN HAVE IN COMMON IS THAT THEY BELIEVED IN THEMSELVES AND THEIR ACTIONS. THEY DIDN'T LET THE DOUBT OF THEIR CAPABILITIES CLOUD THEIR MIND AND STOP THEIR SUCCESS.

**REMEMBER, NO ONE KNOWS EVERYTHING!** JUST BECAUSE YOU DON'T KNOW SOMETHING NOW DOESN'T MEAN YOU CAN'T LEARN AND WON'T GET BETTER WITH TIME. DON'T LOOSE CONFIDENCE IN YOURSELF JUST BECAUSE IT DIDN'T WORK OUT THE FIRST TIME!

**WHAT DOES SUCCESS MEAN TO YOU?** CELEBRATE THE SMALL WINS JUST AS MUCH AS THE BIG WINS. TAKING A STEP BACK TO PAUSE AND REFLECT ON YOUR ACHIEVEMENTS IS THE BIGGEST WAY TO AVOID DOUBT IN YOUR ABILITY AND CAREER JOURNEY.

**YOU'RE A GREAT PERSON REGARDLESS OF WHERE YOU ARE ON THE CAREER LADDER.** YOUR CAREER SUCCESS DOESN'T DEFINE YOU – DON'T LET YOUR DOUBTS TAKE THE JOY OUT OF YOUR WORK AND LIFE BALANCE.

# BESSIE STRINGFIELD

MARCH 5TH, 1911 – FEBRUARY 16TH, 1993
NORTH CAROLINA, USA.

## The Motorcycle Queen of Miami.

AT 16 YEARS OLD, BESSIE STRINGFIELD HAD A MOTORCYCLE AND A DREAM – TO BEGIN A LIFELONG ADVENTURE ON HER MOTORCYCLE AND TRAVEL! IN 1930, AT THE AGE OF 19, SHE BEGAN HER ADVENTURE, BECOMING THE FIRST AFRICAN-AMERICAN WOMAN TO RIDE ACROSS THE UNITED STATES SOLO, AND ALSO TRAVEL ACROSS EUROPE AND SOUTH AMERICA!

HER ADVENTURES WEREN'T WITHOUT STRUGGLE, AND SHE WAS OFTEN DISCRIMINATED AGAINST BECAUSE OF BOTH HER GENDER AND SKIN COLOR, SO SHE FREQUENTLY SLEPT ON HER MOTORCYCLE. FOR MONEY, SHE JOINED CARNIVALS AND PERFORMED STUNTS ON HER TRUSTY VEHICLE!

ALWAYS HAVING A THIRST FOR ADVENTURE, DURING WORLD WAR II SHE ALSO BECAME A COURIER FOR THE US ARMY, AND AFTER THIS MOVED TO MIAMI, WHERE SHE QUICKLY BECAME A LOCAL LEGEND, EARNING THE TITLE, 'THE MOTORCYCLE QUEEN OF MIAMI'.

IF THAT'S NOT THE MOST AWESOME NICKNAME IN HISTORY...I DON'T KNOW WHAT IS!

# MARIE COLVIN

JANUARY 12TH, 1956 – FEBRUARY 22ND, 2012

NEW YORK, USA.

## Reported directly from warzones.

MARIE COLVIN WAS A HARDCORE JOURNALIST AND WORKED AS
A FOREIGN AFFAIRS CORRESPONDENT FOR THE SUNDAY TIMES,
REPORTING FROM DANGEROUS WARZONES.

IN 1999 IN EAST TIMOR, SHE SELFLESSLY HELPED SAVE 1,500
WOMEN AND CHILDREN WHO WERE SURROUNDED BY ARMED
INDONESIAN SOLDIERS. MARIE REFUSED TO LEAVE THEM EVEN
THOUGH SHE WAS ABLE TO LEAVE UNHARMED.

WHILE REPORTING ON THE SRI LANKAN CIVIL WAR, MARIE WAS
CAUGHT IN A DEADLY ROCKET-PROPELLED GRENADE BLAST,
AND LOST SIGHT IN ONE OF HER EYES. DESPITE HER HORRIFIC
INJURIES, SHE MANAGED TO MEET HER DEADLINE ON A 3,000
WORD NEWS ARTICLE.

IN 2012, MARIE, PHOTOJOURNALIST RÉMI OCHLIK, AND
PHOTOGRAPHER PAUL CONROY, FEARLESSLY CROSSED INTO
SYRIA TO REPORT ON THE SYRIAN CIVIL WAR. THE TEAM WERE
STRUCK WITH AN EXPLOSIVE DEVICE FILLED WITH NAILS,
ENDING THE LIVES OF BOTH MARIE AND RÉMI. THOUGH THE
SYRIAN GOVERNMENT BLAMED IT ON TERRORISTS, IN 2016, IT
WAS FOUND THAT THE SYRIAN GOVERNMENT WERE TO BLAME
AND HAD ORDERED COLVIN'S ASSASSINATION.

# "THE QUESTION ISN'T WHO IS GOING TO

## *Let Me*

# IT'S WHO IS GOING TO

## *Stop Me.*"

- AYN RAND

# Try new things

BEING A POWERFUL, STRONG-WILLED BADASS
TAKES MORE THAN KICKING SOME ASS.

AMELIA EARHART DIDN'T KNOW SHE LOVED
FLYING UNTIL **SHE DARED TO TRY**, AND THE SAME
GOES FOR YOU. HOW WILL YOU KNOW YOUR TRUE
STRENGTHS AND PASSIONS IF YOU DON'T PUSH
YOURSELF TO **TRY NEW THINGS AND TEST YOUR
LIMITS?**

**FIND SOMETHING YOU LOVE**, AND PUSH YOURSELF
TO BE THE BEST AT IT. NOT ONLY WILL THIS
GIVE YOU YOUR OWN UNIQUE FLAIR, BUT YOUR
CONFIDENCE AND SELF-ESTEEM WILL SOAR HIGH!

# DAME STEPHANIE SHIRLEY

SEPTEMBER 16TH, 1933

DORTMUND, GERMANY.

## Hired 300 women to fight workplace sexism.

IN A MALE DOMINATED WORLD, STEPHANIE SHIRLEY CHALLENGED THIS HEAD ON, AND CREATED A SAFE WORKPLACE FOR HARD-WORKING WOMEN IN ENGLAND!

LOVING MATHEMATICS AND CODING, SHE DECIDED TO FOUND HER VERY OWN SOFTWARE COMPANY – FREELANCE PROGRAMMERS. AFTER EXPERIENCING HUMILIATING SEXISM AND ASSAULT IN THE WORKPLACE BEFORE, SHE DECIDED TO CREATE A SAFE WORKSPACE AND BRING MORE OPPORTUNITIES FOR WOMEN IN BUSINESS. RUNNING HER BUSINESS WITH A TWIST, WITHIN THE FIRST 300 MEMBERS OF STAFF SHE HIRED, ONLY 3 WERE MEN!

WHEN SHE USED HER FULL NAME, NOBODY RESPONDED TO LETTERS, WHICH ONLY CONFIRMED SEXISM IN BUSINESS AT THE TIME. SO DISGUISING HER GENDER BY DONNING THE NAME 'STEVE', SHE WOULD GO ON TO DO BUSINESS WITH MANY MALE-LED COMPANIES.

WHEN THE SEX DISCRIMINATION ACT WAS PASSED, SHE WAS FORCED TO HIRE MORE MEN, BUT WAS APPOINTED AS A DAME AND RECEIVED AN OBE FOR HER SERVICES TO THE I.T. INDUSTRY.

"*I don't*
CARE
*what you think*
ABOUT ME;
*I don't think about*
*you at all!*"

— COCO CHANEL

# Honesty is the best policy

SOMETHING THAT UNITES BADASS WOMEN THROUGH HISTORY IS THEY'RE **UNAPOLOGETICALLY HONEST!** THEY ARE THEMSELVES THROUGH AND THROUGH, AND ARE NOT WILLING TO BEND OR WAVER THAT FOR ANYONE.

AT TIMES, THIS COULD MAKE YOU UNPOPULAR, BUT NOT BEING A PEOPLE PLEASER WILL ACTUALLY DRAW PEOPLE TOWARDS YOU!

**BE HONEST WITH WHAT YOU WANT FROM LIFE**, AND SHAKE ALL EXPECTATIONS OTHER PEOPLE MIGHT PLACE ON YOU. WITH TRUTH AND HONESTY, BOTH WITH YOURSELF AND WITH OTHERS, COMES POWER AND LIBERATION!

**BE REAL, BE HONEST, BE WEIRD**, AND REALIZE THAT HAVING SELF-ASSURANCE IN YOUR DECISIONS, AND BEING TRANSPARENT AND UPFRONT BOTH WITH YOURSELF AND WITH OTHERS, WILL MAKE YOU FALL IN LOVE WITH YOUR UNIQUENESS (AND MAKE OTHERS DO THE SAME!)

SHOWCASE THE REAL YOU, IN WHATEVER FORM THAT MAY TAKE! **WHAT'S MORE BADASS THAN SOMEONE WHO IS AUTHENTICALLY THEMSELVES?**

UNKNOWN BADASS

1884

ARMENIA.

# Defending her home at 106 years old!

IN 1990, ARMENIA AND THE SURROUNDING AREAS
WERE FORCED INTO AN ARMED CONFLICT WITH
AZERBAIJAN, WITH FAMILIES LEAVING THEIR HOMES
AND FLEEING TO SAFETY, BUT NOT THIS BADASS...
AT AN IMPRESSIVE AGE OF 106 YEARS OLD (YES
YOU READ THAT RIGHT), AND ARMED WITH AN AKM
FIREARM, THIS REBEL GRANNY STOOD HER GROUND,
PROTECTING HER HOME AND LIVELIHOOD FROM
INVASION AND THREAT.

LIKELY WITNESSING THE HAMIDIAN MASSACRES
OF 1894-1896 IN HER CHILDHOOD, AND AGAIN IN
HER 30S, SHE MAY HAVE BEEN FAMILIAR WITH THE
FALLOUT OF WAR, AS CONFLICTS IN THE COUNTRY
HAVE BEEN GOING ON ALL HER LIFE.

THOUGH HER IDENTITY IS STILL UNCONFIRMED, ONE
THING'S FOR SURE, YOU DON'T WANT TO MESS WITH
THIS LADY!

# GRACE O'MALLEY

1530 - 1603

UMHAILL, IRELAND.

## Clan leader and fierce pirate.

WITH FIERY IRISH BLOOD RUNNING THROUGH HER VEINS, IT'S NO WONDER THIS FEARLESS BADASS TOOK TO THE DANGEROUS SEAS FOR ADVENTURE!

GRACE O'MALLEY BECAME CHIEF OF HER FATHER'S CLAN WHEN HE DIED, DESPITE HER HAVING A BROTHER, AND FROM THE AGE OF 11, SHE CREATED A CAREER OF PIRACY AND SEAFARING, AT FIRST BY STOWING AWAY ON HER FATHER'S SHIP, BEFORE BEING CAUGHT BY HIM.

A FIERCE LEADER AT SEA, SHE EVENTUALLY COMMANDED 200 MEN, MANAGING TO PROTECT THE WEST OF IRELAND AS A STRONG FIGHTER, RUTHLESS POLITICIAN AND NOTORIOUS PIRATE. HER PILLAGING OF RIVAL SHIPS LEFT GRACE AND HER CLAN RICH, AND SHE CONTROLLED 5 CASTLES AROUND HER HOMELAND.

GRACE FOUGHT FIERCELY AGAINST QUEEN ELIZABETH I'S PLANS TO BUY OUT EVERY IRISH LORD, BUT WAS CAUGHT BY GOVERNOR RICHARD BINGHAM, AND PUNISHED BRUTALLY FOR HER REBELLION. HER WEALTH PLUMMETED, AS SHE USED IT TO ESCAPE THE DEATH PENALTY, BUT SHE CONTINUED TO NEGOTIATE WITH THE QUEEN FOR THE GOOD OF IRELAND.

"Keep your

# HEAD HIGH

and your

# MIDDLE FINGER

higher."

- MEGAN FOX